HISTORY SHOWTIME

VIKINGS

Liza Phipps & Avril Thompson

W
FRANKLIN WATTS
LONDON·SYDNEY

About this book

History Showtime takes an interactive approach to learning history. Alongside the key information about an ancient civilisation are songs for children to perform, crafts to make and games to play. These are brought together at the end of the book by a play about a big event or aspect of the history of the civilization which children can perform themselves, using the crafts they have made over the course of the book as props and including performances of the songs the children have learned.

These icons signpost the different activities:

To enrich the learning experience, music from the book is also available to download online as audio tracks, music scores and lyrics. Visit www. franklinwatts.co.uk/historyshowtime or just scan

 This logo appears where downloadable material is available.

First published in 2013 by
Franklin Watts
338 Euston Road
London NW1 3BH

Franklin Watts Australia
Level 17/207 Kent Street
Sydney NSW 2000

Text, lyrics and music copyright © Liza Phipps and Avril Thompson 2013
Avril Thompson and Liza Phipps have asserted their right to be identified as the Authors of this Work

ISBN: 978 1 4451 1483 5
Dewey classification number: 948.'022

Editor: Julia Bird
Designer: Rita Storey

Photo acknowledgements:
Almgren/Dreamstime: 21t. Natalia Antonova/Shutterstock: 10b. Art Gallery Collection/Alamy: 8b. Robert Bird/Alamy: 11b. Werner Forman Archive: 1, 7t, 13c, 16b, 18bl, 18tr. Cindy Hopkins/ Alamy: 5b, 11t. Doug Houghton/Alamy: 21b. Interfoto/Alamy: 18tl. Veronika Kachalkina/Shutterstock: 19t, 28b. Russell Kaye/Getty Images: front cover main., 8t. Maurice Lee Choong Min/istockphoto: 10t. Jonathan Mitchell/Alamy: 24b. Alan Morrison/Shutterstock: 12t. Orkney Museum/Kirkwall: 13t. Igor Risselev/Alamy: 12b. Bruce Rolff/ Shutterstock: front cover r. Anna Stasevska/Shutterstock: 23t. Bjorn Stefanson/Shutterstock: 4t. Doug Steley/Alamy: 6b. Ullsteinbild/Topfoto: 6t, 15t. Universal Images Group/De Agostini/Alamy: 24t. Visual Arts Library/Alamy: 16t. Marilyn Volan/Shutterstock: front cover c. wikipedia: 14-15b. York Archaeological Trust: 14t, 14c, 22t

With thanks to our model Shania-Mae Phipps and to the choir of the Jackie Palmer Stage School, High Wycombe.

Every attempt has been made to clear copyright. Should there be any inadvertent omission, please apply to the publisher for rectification.

Franklin Watts is a division of Hachette Children's Books, an Hachette UK company.
www.hachette.co.uk

Contents

Words in **bold** can be found in
the glossary on page 31.

The Viking age

The Vikings were **invaders** who lived over a thousand years ago. They came from Scandinavia, from the countries we now know as Denmark, Norway and Sweden.

Raiders

The Viking age began in the 8th century CE when shiploads of Viking warriors began **raiding** neighbouring countries. They seized goods, money and treasure, and killed or captured anyone unlucky enough to get in their way.

The Vikings came from the cold, mountainous lands of Scandinavia.

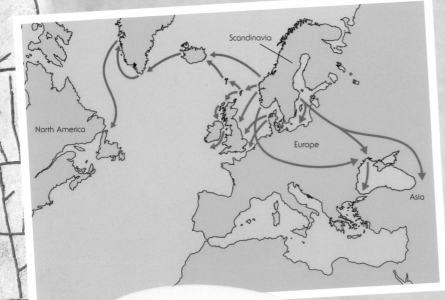

The Vikings travelled far into Europe and Asia, as this map shows. One famous Viking, Leif Eriksson, even reached the coast of North America.

Settling down

The Vikings travelled far and wide. Their raids took them to new places, where they gradually set up successful **trade** links. Over time, some Vikings settled in some of these new lands. They were mostly farmers and these lands had better soil and warmer weather than their homelands. **Communities** and towns began to grow.

TRUE!

The word Viking means 'pirate raid' in the old **Norse** language.

We are the Vikings

The Vikings travelled all over the world, discovering new lands. Sing a song to celebrate their courage!

♩ = 108   *Marching*

Raid-ers from the North,   stran-gers from the sea,   Sail-ing in our
Raid-ers from the North,   land of ice and snow,   Ro-cky cliffs and

long-ships,   Pir-ates from a-far,   land-ing on the shore,   Fast and fierce and free!
moun-tains,   Launch-ing our a-ttacks,   hear our ba-ttle cries,   Ev'-ry-where we go!

We are the Vi-kings,   ter-ri-ble Vi-kings!   We are the brav-est of the brave,
We are the Vi-kings,   ter-ri-ble Vi-kings!   We are the rough-est of the rough,

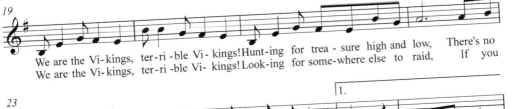

We ne-ver care how bad-ly we be-have,   We are figh-ters from the cra-dle to the grave!
E-ven our re-pu-ta-tion is e-nough,   We get go-ing when the go-ing's get-ting tough!

We are the Vi-kings,   ter-ri-ble Vi-kings!Hunt-ing for trea-sure high and low,   There's no
We are the Vi-kings,   ter-ri-ble Vi-kings!Look-ing for some-where else to raid,   If you

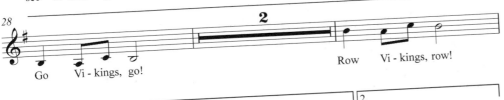

1.
point in trying to hide it,   If we find it we'll grab it and go!   Go Vi-kings, go!
see us head-ing for you   Then it's time to be ve-ry a-

Go   Vi-kings, go!   Row   Vi-kings, row!

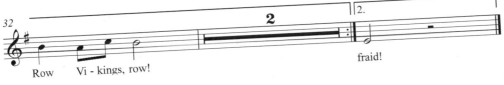

2.
Row   Vi-kings, row!   fraid!

Viking warriors

The Vikings were famous for being fierce and fearless in battle. They fought for a local leader, who rewarded them by sharing treasures taken on their raids.

This painting shows what a Viking raiding party might have looked like.

Swift attack

Viking raids were sudden and brutal. The Vikings set out at the beginning of summer when the snow and ice melted, allowing them to travel. They swooped in their ships into a bay or up a river and attacked without warning, giving their **victims** little or no chance to defend themselves.

Invaders

The Vikings came ashore in small groups and fought on foot, armed with weapons such as a **longsword**, axe or spear, knife and shield. They were ferocious in battle, killing those who got in their way and taking many prisoners to keep as **slaves**.

TRUE!

The Vikings targeted **monasteries** and churches on their raids. They even stole church bells!

An actor dressed as a Viking warrior, ready for battle.

Make a Viking helmet

To protect themselves in battle, Viking warriors wore helmets made of leather or iron. Viking helmets did not have horns!

1. Cut 8 strips of card 29.7cm by 4cm.

2. Join two strips with double-sided tape to make a cross.

3. Repeat step 2 with all of the remaining strips. Lay the crosses on top of each other with the centres touching to form a circle (above). Stick the centres together with double-sided tape.

4. Cut a strip of card to fit around your head. Join the edges to make a band. Carefully push the joined-up strips through the head band to make the helmet shape. Stick the ends of the strips to the head band.

5. Cut out the shape of the eye and nose piece using the template available at www.franklinwatts.co.uk/historyshowtime.

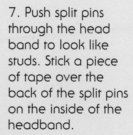

6. Glue or tape the eye and nose piece to the underneath of the head band. Paint or spray the helmet silver.

7. Push split pins through the head band to look like studs. Stick a piece of tape over the back of the split pins on the inside of the headband.

Your helmet is ready to wear!

Vikings at sea

The Vikings were successful at sea because they were excellent sailors, boat builders and **navigators**.

Boat designers

The Vikings built special warships, called longships, that were light, fast and shallow. They could be sailed up rivers and landed on beaches. The Vikings also built **cargo** ships, which were wider and heavier and more suitable for carrying goods over longer distances for trade.

A **replica** of a Viking longship. The sailors are using long oars to row.

At sea

Each ship had a large sail which could be taken down in stormy weather and spread over the boat to shelter the crew. The ship also had oars so that it could be rowed when the wind dropped or the boat was close to the shore. It was steered by a special board, which was like a great big oar. The Vikings sailed hundreds of kilometres in these boats, keeping close to the shore whenever possible. They would use the position of the Sun by day and the stars by night to find their way.

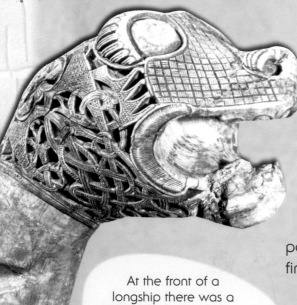

At the front of a longship there was a **figurehead** of a dragon or other scary monster to frighten the enemy!

TRUE!

The word starboard, meaning the right-hand side of a ship, comes from the Viking word 'styra', meaning 'to steer'.

Sea Song

The Vikings told stories and sang songs to keep their spirits up at sea. Maybe they sang a song like this one?

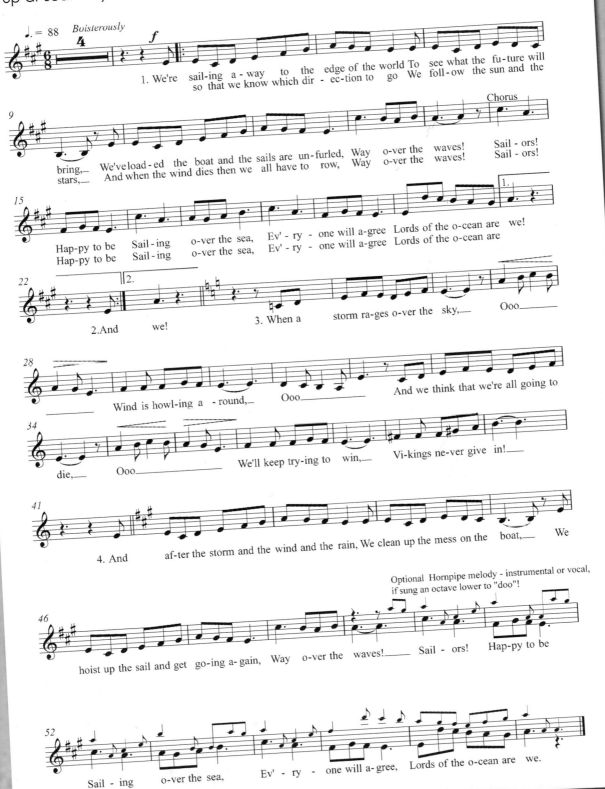

At home

When they were not at sea, the Vikings lived by farming and hunting. Women mainly looked after the household and children.

Work

Most Vikings were farmers. They grew vegetables including onions, cabbages and beans, and crops such as oats, barley and rye. They kept animals to provide them with meat, milk, eggs and cheese, leather and wool for clothing and feathers, which were used to stuff pillows and mattresses. The Vikings also fished and went hunting for meat and furs.

Fish were hung up on racks to dry, or smoked or salted to **preserve** them during the cold, dark winter.

Young Vikings

Viking children didn't go to school. Instead, boys helped around the farm and girls learned the skills needed to run the household. In particular, girls learned to cook and how to spin wool and **weave** it into cloth to be made into clothes.

TRUE!

The Vikings ate seagulls and would climb cliffs to raid their nests!

Longhouses

Vikings lived in rectangular houses up to 30 metres long called longhouses. The walls were built of local materials, usually wood or stone, and the roof was often covered with **turf**.

Inside

Inside the longhouse there was one main room for living and sleeping, with a large fireplace in the middle for cooking. It was dark and smoky, as the hole in the roof above the fire did not let smoke escape very efficiently. There was not much furniture. The walls were lined with benches, which were used for sitting on by day and sleeping on by night. Belongings were kept in large chests. The only other large piece of furniture would be the family's **loom**.

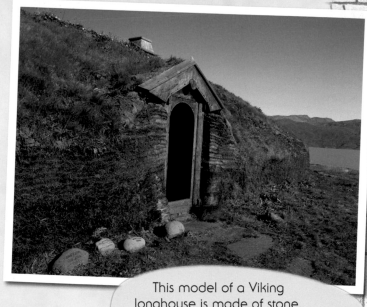

This model of a Viking longhouse is made of stone, with turf growing on the roof.

TRUE!

In winter, farm animals lived inside with the family. It must have been a bit smelly!

The inside of a Viking longhouse would have looked like this.

Dress and appearance

The Vikings dressed mainly for comfort and warmth in the harsh climate of Scandinavia, and their clothes were quite simple.

Women

Women wore a long **linen** underdress with a sleeveless wool overdress, which was held together at the shoulder with two oval brooches. A length of chain or string of beads between the brooches was used to hang keys or other small tools on (see page 17).

Men and children

Men wore tight wool trousers with a pair of linen **breeches** underneath, and a long-sleeved, open-necked tunic which often reached down to their knees, with a belt tied round their waist. Both men and women wore soft leather boots or shoes and heavy cloaks in cold weather. Children would dress in the same sort of clothes as their parents.

A woman dressed in traditional Viking clothes.

Viking dress was warm and practical.

The Vikings used 'ironing boards' like this one made of whalebone. Clothes were rubbed with a stone or lump of glass to smooth them.

Grooming

The Vikings have a name for being dirty, rough people, but in fact they were quite particular about their clothing and appearance. Most would have a bath or **sauna** once a week and changed their clothes quite frequently for the time. They used mashed conkers, mixed with water then squeezed and left to dry, as a kind of soap.

A Viking comb made of bone, decorated with an animal head (left) and a human head (right).

TRUE!

Vikings carried tiny spoons for scooping wax out of their ears!

Hair

The Vikings paid particular attention to their hair. Combs made of bone or antler have been discovered by **archaeologists** at ancient Viking settlements. Viking men often wore their hair long and usually had beards. Women wore their hair long and loose, though they often braided it or wore a band or scarf over it.

Make-up

The Vikings liked to wear make-up, particularly around their eyes. They made their own make-up from the juices of berries mixed with mud and animal fat to protect them from sunburn.

Entertainment

The Vikings worked hard, but they loved to have fun too, and particularly enjoyed sports.

Outdoors

The Vikings enjoyed games and competitions. In summer they spent as much time as possible outdoors, where they had swimming, rowing and horse-riding races, and wrestling and weightlifting contests. In winter they went skiing, iceskating and sledging.

Ice skates were made of bone or antler and attached to leather shones.

These musical instruments include a bone pipe (top right), wooden pan pipe (middle) and part of a **lyre** (left).

Inside

Indoor activities included singing, dancing and making music, and playing games such as chess which had been brought back from journeys to the Middle East. The Vikings also played a complicated board game called hnefetafl which was invented by their **ancestors**.

This is a Viking game called Kubb, which was a bit like bowling.

Toys

Children played with toys such as model boats and wooden dolls. Boys also had wooden swords and other weapons, and were expected to start practising to be a warrior from an early age.

Feasts

On special occasions, such as festivals or when men returned home from their travels, the Vikings enjoyed holding great feasts. These occasions were a good excuse to eat too much and get drunk! The Vikings would be entertained by **professional** entertainers or storytellers (see page 22).

TRUE!

Vikings gave each other funny nicknames, such as 'Harald Hairy Breeches'!

This set of Viking chess pieces was found on the Isle of Lewis in Scotland. They are made of walrus ivory and whale bone.

Crafts and jewellery

The Vikings were skilled craftsmen and many of their everyday items were beautifully made and decorated.

At war

Viking ships were extremely well crafted. They were made from overlapping planks of wood, fastened with iron **rivets**. This made them strong, but also flexible enough to ride the ocean waves. Viking weapons were carefully made from the strongest materials, such as iron, and beautifully decorated.

At home

Viking cloth was woven on a loom and decorated with **embroidered** borders. Wooden and stone buildings were carved with pictures that showed scenes of everyday life, or told stories of the Viking gods (see page 18). Jewellery, bowls and plates, and even tools were covered with beautiful patterns and designs.

Trade

The Vikings used their craft skills for trade. During their travels, they exchanged items such as furs, fish, timber, walrus ivory and their own home-made crafts for gold and silver, wine, exotic spices, silk, glass and other luxury items from distant countries.

A collection of Viking objects including swords, a spearhead (left) and a stirrup (middle).

TRUE!

A Viking warrior's sword was so valuable that he would give it a name such as 'leg-biter' and it would be buried with him when he died.

A Viking pendant made of bronze.

16

Make a pair of Viking brooches

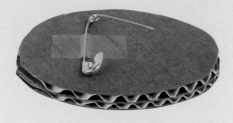

1. Draw an oval shape on thick card. Cut this shape out 4 times.

2. Glue 2 ovals together to make a brooch. Repeat with the other two ovals.

3. When the glue has dried, use a small piece of sticky tape to fasten a safety pin onto the back of each brooch. Try to place your pin slightly above half-way up your brooch so that it will lie properly.

4. Decorate your brooch by making patterns on the surface. You could make holes using a compass point; coil some string or cord and glue it on; glue a button in the middle or make patterns by sticking on some small beads or small balls of clay or foil.

5. Use a sharp instrument, such as a compass point, to make a hole through each brooch near the bottom. Spray or paint your brooches with gold paint and leave them to dry.

6. Tie one end of a length of cord through the hole in one brooch. Thread some beads onto the cord. Tie the other end through the hole in the other brooch and pin them both to your clothes.

Gods and goddesses

The first Vikings were **pagans**, and worshipped many gods. They prayed to different gods for their protection and for help with daily life. Later, many became **Christians**.

Great gods and goddesses

Odin

Odin was the chief god and god of war and magic. He only had one eye, having traded the other in for the gift of wisdom. He lived in Valhalla (see page 21).

Thor was the god of thunder, armed with his mighty hammer, Mjollnir. Thor was a very popular god who was believed to bring good luck. Many Vikings wore a model hammer pendant round their neck to keep them safe.

Frey and Freya were twin brother and sister. Frey was the god of nature and sacrifices were made to him to ensure good crops. Freya was the goddess of love and beauty. She was believed to love gold and wore a special golden necklace.

Loki was only a half-god, but a very important character in Viking stories. He was a great joker and entertainer, but was also believed to be untrustworthy. He was known as the 'shapeshifter' because he wore different disguises.

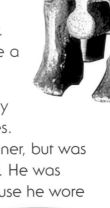

Thor

Freya

TRUE!
The Vikings believed that the world was created by a giant called Ymir.

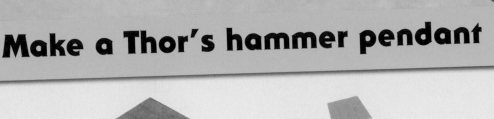

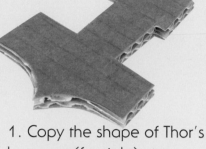

1. Copy the shape of Thor's hammer (far right) onto some thick card. It should be about 9 cm tall and 7 cm wide.

2. Repeat and cut out both shapes. Glue them together. This is the pendant.

A replica Thor's hammer pendant

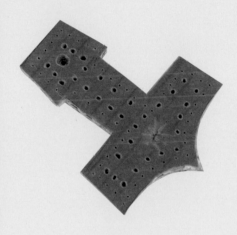

4. Spray or paint your pendant with gold or silver paint and leave it to dry.

3. Use a sharp instrument such as a compass point to make a hole through the top of the pendant. Decorate your pendant by making patterns on the surface. You could make dots using a compass point or coil some string or cord and glue it on. Use some of the pictures in this book for ideas.

5. Cut a length of cord that is long enough to go over your head. Thread one end of the cord through the hole and tie both ends together. Your pendant is ready!

Thor's Hammer

One popular Viking story told how the evil giant Thrym stole the magic hammer belonging to Thor. Loki helped to get it back again after Freya refused to marry the giant to ensure the hammer's return.

Viking funerals

Funeral **ceremonies** were important to the Vikings. They were often buried with their most treasured belongings, in case they needed them in the **afterlife**.

Special stones

Less wealthy people were often buried in the ground, surrounded by stones arranged in the shape of a ship. **Memorial** stones carved with **runes** (see page 23) were put up to remember them.

A Viking burial ground in Sweden. The stones have been laid out to look like a longship.

A replica longship is set alight at a Viking festival held on the Shetland Islands in Scotland.

Ship burials

Wealthy Vikings were sometimes buried in their ships. The body was laid in the boat surrounded by their personal possessions. The ship was then set alight and pushed out to sea.

Valhalla

Valhalla was the hall of the Viking gods. Vikings believed that all warriors who were killed in battle would go to Valhalla to live a life of pleasure and luxury forever after.

How do we know?

We have learned about the Vikings from **excavating** sites where they used to live. Stories, songs and carvings also tell us a lot about the Viking age.

Digging up the past

Much of what we know about the Vikings comes from objects that have been dug up by archaeologists. From what they find, historians can work out how people lived, where and how they travelled, what sort of things they made, what they believed and how they buried their dead.

Storytelling

The Vikings enjoyed listening to tales told during the long, dark winter nights. These stories, known as sagas, told of ancient heroes, gods and goddesses, giants, elves and magic. Few Vikings could read or write so the stories were not written down. Instead, they were remembered and passed from **generation** to generation. Eventually an Icelander called Snorri Sturlsson wrote the sagas down in the 13th century. These sagas give valuable details about how the Vikings lived.

Archaeologists have uncovered the ruins of the Viking town of Jorvik below the city centre of York in England.

TRUE!

By excavating the contents of Viking toilets, archaeologists have been able to work out what Vikings ate!

Runes

The Vikings did not have ink or paper and the only form of writing was a basic alphabet of 16 letters called runes. It was made up of straight lines so it was suitable for carving with a hammer and **chisel** on wood or stone. It was used to write simple messages, such as on memorial stones to record who had died. Many rune stones have survived across Scandinavia. They tell us more about the lives and deaths of the Vikings.

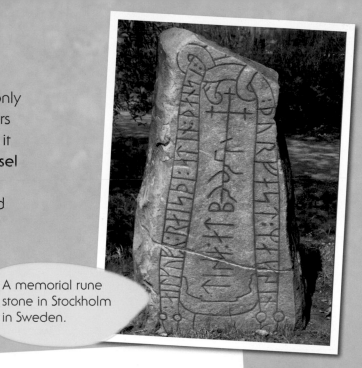

A memorial rune stone in Stockholm in Sweden.

Runes

Use the letters of this simple runic alphabet to write a simple message to a friend. See if your friend can read it!

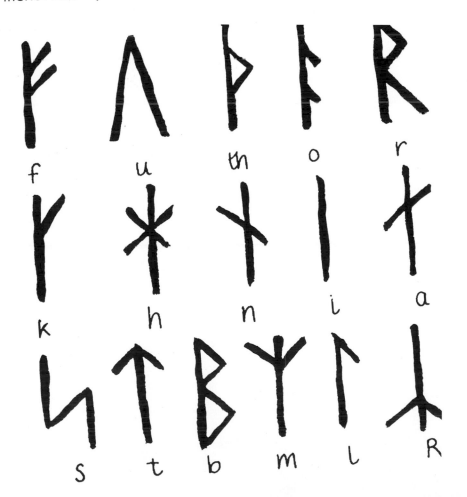

The Viking Legacy

The Vikings are most famous for being invaders and warriors. But they should also be remembered for their achievements.

A golden age

Between the 8th and the 11th centuries CE, the Vikings established an **empire** that stretched from their **native** Scandinavia right across the Atlantic Ocean to North America and south into the Mediterranean. They managed this just with sailing ships, and their **legacy** remains wherever they went.

Settlements

The early Vikings established settlements in northern Britain, Ireland, the Faroe Islands, Iceland and Greenland. Many place names in these countries are of Norse or Viking origin such as Reykjavik in Iceland, and York (Jorvik) in England.

This silver coin made in the trading town of Hedeby has survived to remind us of the Viking age.

TRUE!
Many Viking words exist today. They include Thurs (Thors) day, egg, legs, sister, husband, happy, ill, sky, heaven and lake.

New beginnings

Eventually, the countries that the Vikings raided became stronger. Over time, they drove out the Viking raiders. Those Vikings who stayed behind adapted to a more peaceful life in their new home.

Ruins, like this one of a longhouse in the Shetland Islands are a legacy of the Viking age.

When Vikings Sail over the Sea

The Vikings are remembered as great sailors and explorers.
Sing a song to remember their adventures!

1. Sail - ing in - to the fu - ture,___ From rai - ders to
2. Sail - ing in - to the sun - set,___ Ex - plor - ers, we're

tra - ders are we, Saying fare - well to the old life,___ We're liv - ing ad -
brave and we're bold, Foll - ow - ing the ex - am - ple___ Of her - oes from

ven - tur - ous - ly! Free - dom to roam, make a new home___ For our chil -
sa - gas of old. Mak - ing our mark, out of the dark___ Of the North -

dren to se - ttle for - ev - er, Cre - at - ing their own des - tin - y!___
lands, be - yond___ the hor - i - zon, We're watch - ing our new lives un - fold!___

New cul - tures, new lang - uag - es, new ways of li - ving,

That's what the fu - ture can be,___ Neigh - bours to - ge - ther, re - ceiv - ing and

giv - ing,___ Hap - py when Vi - kings sail o - ver the sea!

Hap - py when Vi - kings sail o - ver the sea!

A Viking Adventure

By the end of the 9th century CE, many Viking families were leaving their homes in Scandinavia. They settled in warmer, more fertile lands further south, which had been discovered by the early raiders and explorers. This is the story of one group of families seeking a better way of life across the sea.

Cast

- **Olaf** boat owner and leader of the group
- **Inga** his wife
- **Bjorn** aged 11
- **Lars** aged 8
- **Freya** aged 6
- **Sigrid** Olaf's elderly mother

Men, women and children, neighbours and friends of Olaf and his family, who are travelling with them.

Props

You will need the following items:

- *Some bundles and sacks of cargo*
- *Blankets, cloaks or shawls*
- *A Thor's hammer pendant (See page 19)*

You could make a sail for your boat by tying two long poles together in a T-shape and attaching a sheet to the horizontal pole. Get two people to hold the sheet up as the boat is sailing.

SONG: **'We are the Vikings'**

(During the song we see Olaf and his family and friends loading their boat with cargo ready to set sail. They are dressed in Viking clothes with warm cloaks and blankets wrapped round them to protect them from bad weather during their voyage from their home by a mountainous fjord to a new life in eastern England.)

Olaf: Right, I think that's everything. We need to get going before the tide turns. Erik, Harald, can you get ready to hoist the sail and the rest of us will have to row till we get out of the bay.

Inga:	Children, you need to sit down out of the way at the back there.
Bjorn:	Father, can I row too?
Olaf:	Another day, Bjorn. We need to row hard now until we can catch the wind and fill the sail. What you can do is stand up at the front and keep a sharp look out for any hidden rocks ahead of us. Mind you shout loudly if you see anything.
Man:	*(Steering at the back)* And point to it as well, lad, so that I can steer away from it.
Lars:	Is it true that we're going to be raiding and fighting?

(The adults laugh.)

Man:	We hope not, young Lars. That's not part of the plan!
Lars:	*(Disappointed)* Oh! Grandma said we'd be bound to do at least one raid!
Olaf:	Mother! What have you been saying to the children?
Sigrid:	Nothing! I was just telling them how your father never went on an expedition without doing at least one raid. He wasn't afraid to fight. He was a real man!
Olaf:	Of course he was, Mother, and we're not afraid to fight either if we have to. But times are changing. Thanks to people like him we now know that there are wonderful places out there where we can make a new life for ourselves and our children. Good farming land, a warm climate, daylight all year round and some of our own people already settled there. It's too good a chance to miss.
Man:	Last summer when we landed in England, we found lots of flat land with rich soil where we can grow crops and feed our animals all year round. The sea never freezes and we can always find fresh water.
Man:	And there's a great city called Jorvik (*say 'Yorvik'*) where we can trade our goods and the things we make.
Olaf:	That's where we're heading, Mother, and there should be no reason to fight. We can settle in comfort amongst our

own people who speak our language and share our customs.

Sigrid: Huh! Your father would never have left our homeland, no matter how hard life was. He was a real man!

Inga: *(Trying to be patient with the old lady)* We *know* that, but that's in the past. And we shall miss our old life in many ways, but this is for the best. It's going to be a great adventure!

SONG: 'Sea Song'

(During the song there is a storm and everybody huddles down until it passes.)

Olaf: Is everybody all right? That was a nasty storm. Fortunately the boat seems to have survived it.

Man: Thanks to the skills of Magnus, our master boat-builder here.

(Applause for Magnus)

Freya: I still feel sick!

Inga: Just take some deep breaths of fresh air and you'll be fine.

Sigrid: Be brave, Freya. A true Viking doesn't give in to a little thing like sea sickness!

Freya: *(Miserably)* Yes Grandma.

Sigrid: We all have to be brave when things get tough!

Bjorn: *(Cheekily)* Just like our grandfather!

(Giggling from the other children who are a bit too used to hearing about how brave Sigrid's husband was!)

Sigrid: That's right, Bjorn. In fact that reminds me, I've been meaning to give you this. It used to be your grandfather's. He always wore it to bring him good luck so now seems like a good time for you to have it.

(She hands him the Thor's hammer pendant. The children gather round to have a look.)

Bjorn: What is it, Grandma?

Sigrid: It's the magic hammer of the great god Thor. As you're the oldest grandson it should pass to you now.

Freya: Who's the great god Thor, Grandma?

Lars: Everybody knows who Thor is, silly. He's the god of thunder and he brings us good fortune.

Sigrid: Have you heard the story about what happened when the hammer was stolen by the evil giant Thrym?

Lars: No.

Sigrid: And how he said he would only give it back if the beautiful goddess Freya would marry him?

Freya: Freya? That's my name!

Inga: That's right. That's why we named you Freya, because you're beautiful!

(Freya looks happy and proud, sea sickness forgotten, until the younger boys start jeering and making sick noises.)

Inga: Be quiet, boys, that's not kind!

Bjorn: Tell us the story, Grandma, please. Your stories are really interesting.

Sigrid: Thank you. Well this is quite a funny story. It's all about how Loki the joker, Thor's friend, had a really unusual idea to help him to defeat the giant and get his hammer back again.

SONG: **'Thor's Hammer'**

(During the song, the actors all act out the story, taking on the parts of the characters in the story.)

Lookout: Land ahead!

(Everyone jumps up and looks to the front of the boat.)

Woman: Are you sure? I can't see anything.

Olaf: That's probably because it's flat land.

Child: Flat land? No mountains?

Olaf: No mountains! No rocks, not many islands, just sandy shores, beautiful flat green grassland and lots of woodland.

Man: We must be nearing land. Look, there are some leaves and bits of wood floating in the water.

Bjorn: I can see it! Just a thin grey line on the horizon, but it's definitely land.

Inga: We've made it! Nine days and nights and thanks to the gods, we've made it safely across the sea. I wonder where we are.

Man: I reckon we're not very far from where we landed last year. What do you think, Olaf?

Olaf: I agree. It looks pretty much like what we saw then. But wherever it is, this is where our new life begins. It won't be easy to begin with. We'll have to find somewhere to live and build ourselves houses and dig the fields to plant crops. But in its own way I reckon it's going to be just as heroic an adventure as our ancestors going raiding in the olden days.

SONG: **'When Vikings Sail Over the Sea'**

Glossary

afterlife - a new life that begins after death

ancestor - someone from who you are descended

archaeologist - someone who digs up objects to find out about the past

breeches - trousers

cargo - the goods carried on a ship

ceremonies - special occasions, such as weddings or funerals

chisel - a small tool used for carving

Christians - followers of the teachings of Jesus Christ

communities - groups of people who live together in a place

embroidered - covered in decorative stitching

empire - all the land under the control of a race of people

excavate - to dig up

figurehead - the figure or statue found at the front of a ship

generation - all the people in a group or country who are of a similar age

invaders - to enter a place by force and take it over

legacy - something that has survived from the past

linen - a tough cloth woven from flax

longsword - a type of sword with a long, narrow blade and double-handed hilt

loom - a large frame used for weaving yarn into cloth

lyre - a stringed instrument

memorial - a way of remembering someone who has died

monastery - a place where religious men called monks live

native - to come from a place

navigator - someone who can find their way, or navigate, on a journey

Norse - an old name for people from Scandinavia and for their language

pagan - someone who doesn't follow any of the major religions, but worships their own gods

preserve - to add a substance, such as salt, to something to stop it rotting

professional - when you are paid to do a task

raid - a sudden attack

replica - a copy of something

rivet - a metal pin used to join things together

runes - the letters of an ancient alphabet

sauna - a hot steam bath

slave - a person who is forced to work for someone else

trade - buying and selling goods

turf - the top layer of a field, made of grass and earth

victim - someone who suffers harm

weave - to make cloth by joining together bits of yarn

Index

Find out more

http://www.bbc.co.uk/schools/primaryhistory/vikings/
A fun child-friendly site with lots of links and activities to enrich the learning experience.

http://www.educationscotland.gov.uk/scotlandshistory/britonsgaelsvikings/vikings/index.asp
A well-presented site giving plenty of information on the Viking invasions of Britain. Includes videos, games and lots of other useful links.

Note to parents and teachers: every effort has been made by the Publishers to ensure that these websites are suitable for children, that they are of the highest educational value, and that they contain no inappropriate or offensive material. However, because of the nature of the Internet, it is impossible to guarantee that the contents of these sites will not be altered. We strongly advise that Internet access is supervised by a responsible adult.